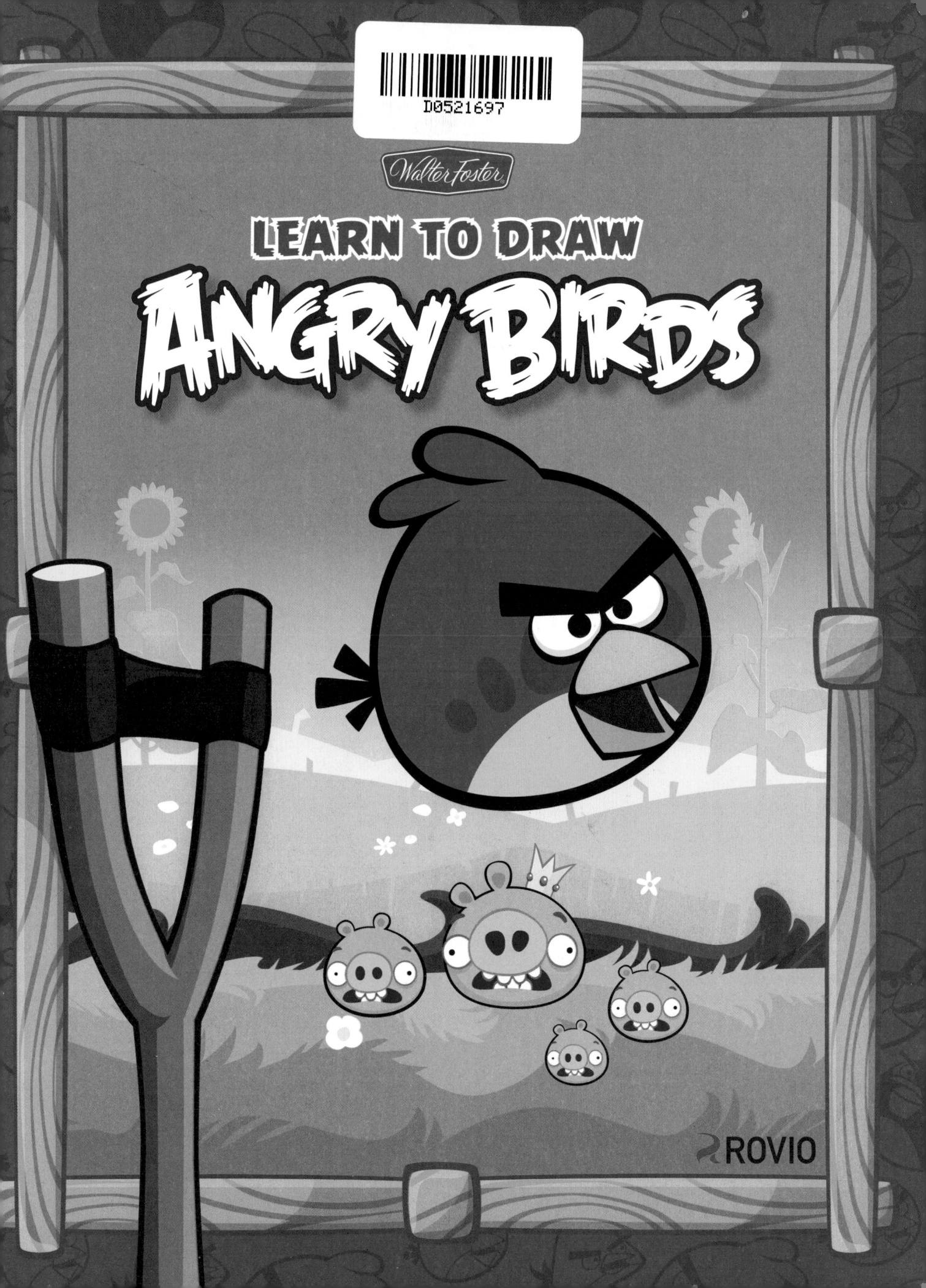
D0521697
Walter Foster
LEARN TO DRAW
ANGRY BIRDS
ROVIO

Step-by-step illustrations by Kristina Marroquin-Burr

© 2009-2012 Rovio Entertainment Ltd.
Angry Birds and Rovio are trademarks of Rovio Entertainment Ltd. All rights reserved.

1 3 5 7 9 10 8 6 4 2

TABLE OF CONTENTS

Introducing the Angry Birds 4

Tools & Materials 5

How to Use this Book 6

Size Chart 7

Red 8

Chuck 14

Bomb 18

Matilda 22

The Blues 24

Minion Pigs 26

Corporal Pig 28

King Pig 30

The End 32

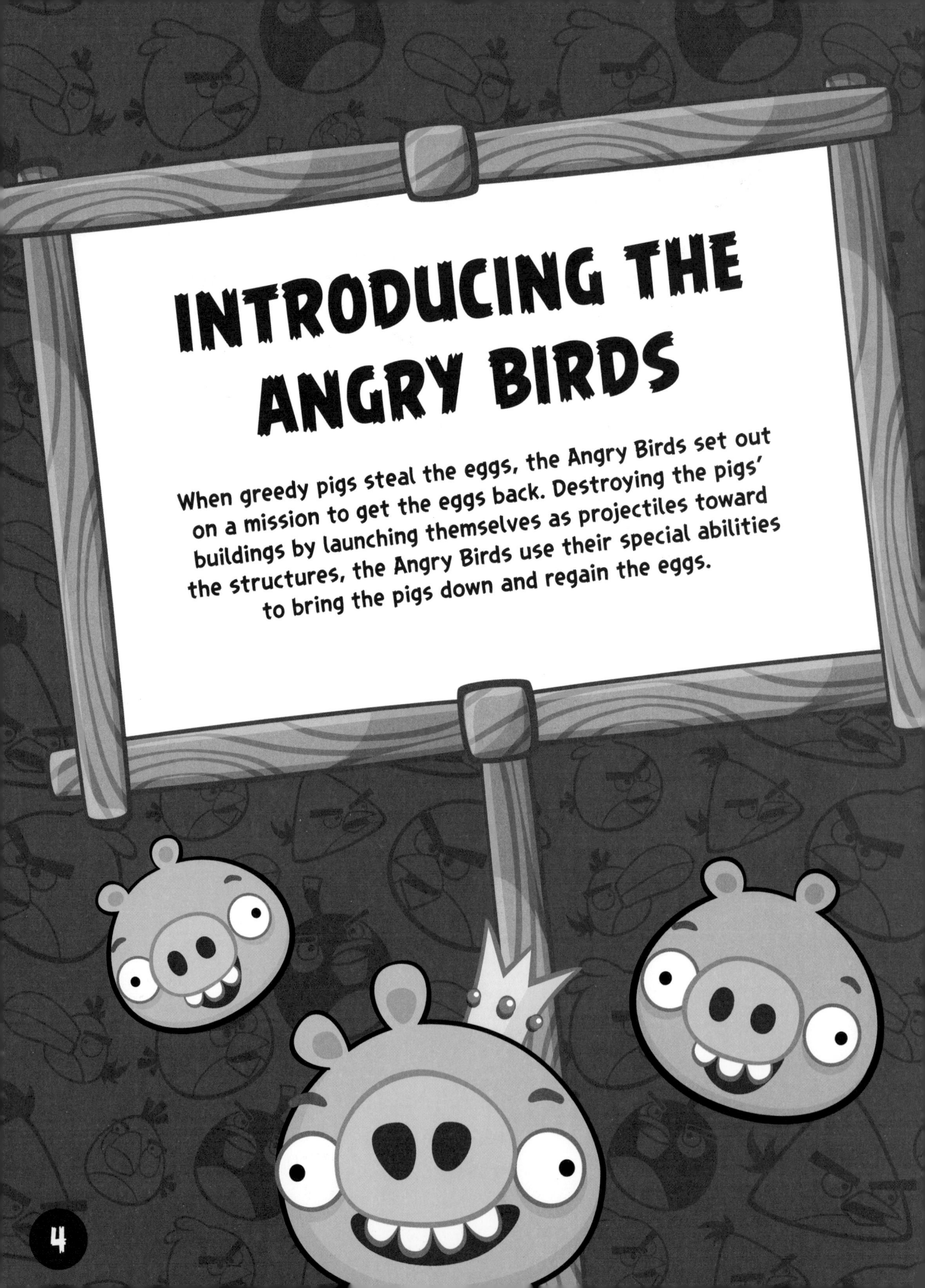

INTRODUCING THE ANGRY BIRDS

When greedy pigs steal the eggs, the Angry Birds set out on a mission to get the eggs back. Destroying the pigs' buildings by launching themselves as projectiles toward the structures, the Angry Birds use their special abilities to bring the pigs down and regain the eggs.

TOOLS & MATERIALS

Before you begin drawing, you will need to gather the right tools. Start with a regular pencil, an eraser, and a pencil sharpener. When you're finished with your drawing, you can bring your characters to life by adding color with crayons, colored pencils, markers, or even paint!

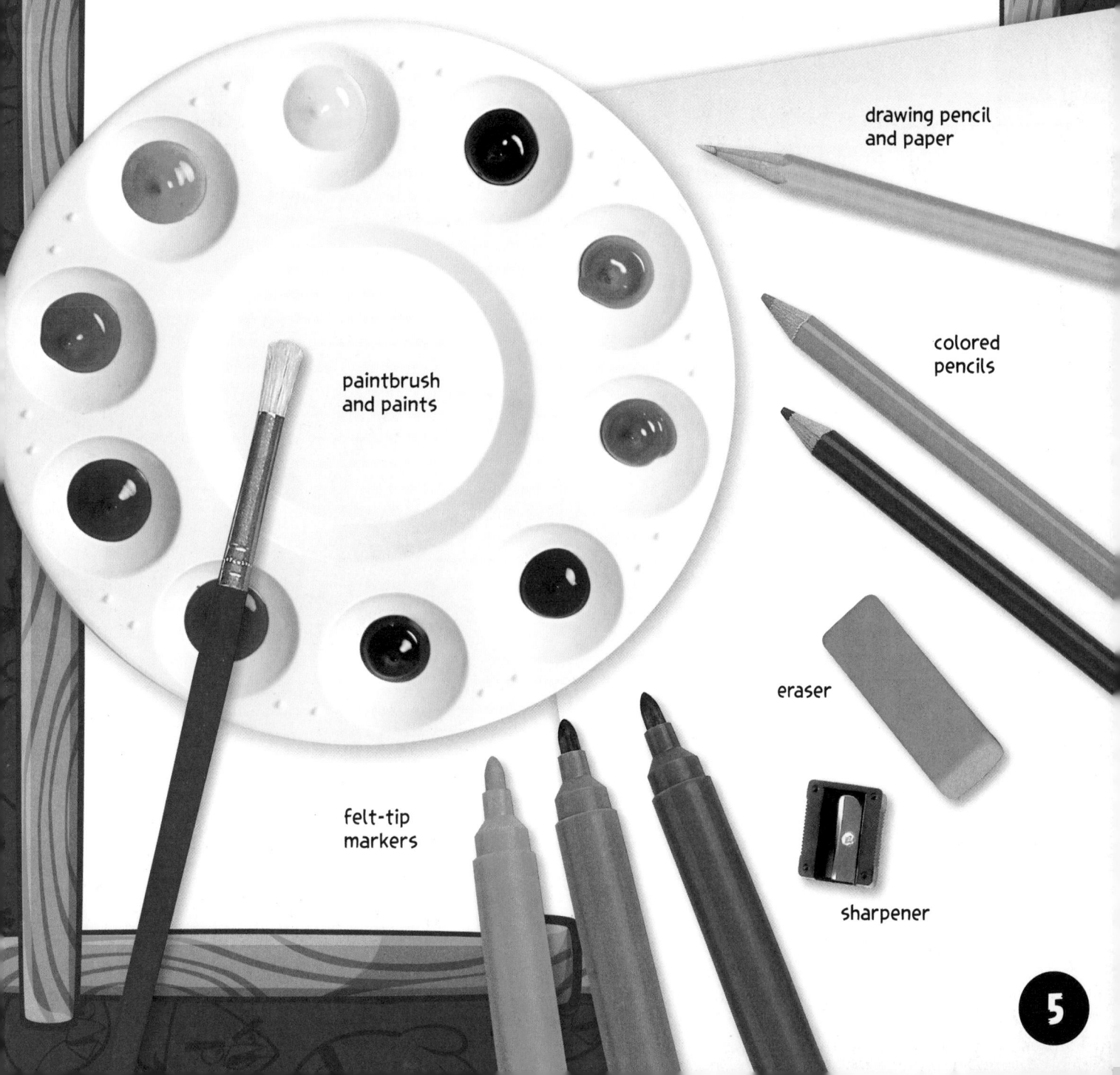

HOW TO USE THIS BOOK

Professional artists draw characters in steps. The key is to start with simple shapes and gradually add the details. The blue lines will help guide you through the process.

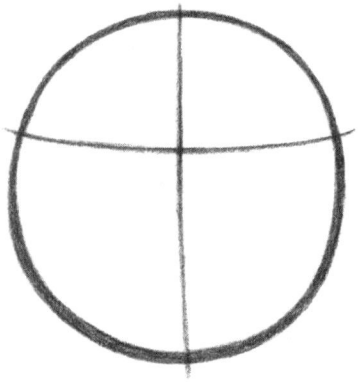

1 First you'll draw guidelines to help position the character's features.

2 Next, you'll add the details step by step.

3 When you finish adding the details, erase your guidelines. Then darken your final sketch lines with a pen or a marker.

SIZE CHART

Red
The Blues
Chuck
Matilda
Bomb
Minion Pig Small
Minion Pig Medium
Corporal Pig
King Pig

RED

Red is the iconic hero of Angry Birds and is instantly recognized everywhere in the world. The striking red plume and yellow beak of the fluffy Red bird really set him apart in a crowd.

4
5
Do you feel lucky, pig?

1
2
3

4
5
A is for Angry.

1
2
3

4
5
LOL!

CHUCK

Similar in size to Red, the almost cone-shaped Yellow bird, Chuck, speeds through the air like a bullet. The streamlined Yellow bird is slimmer than its Red brother.

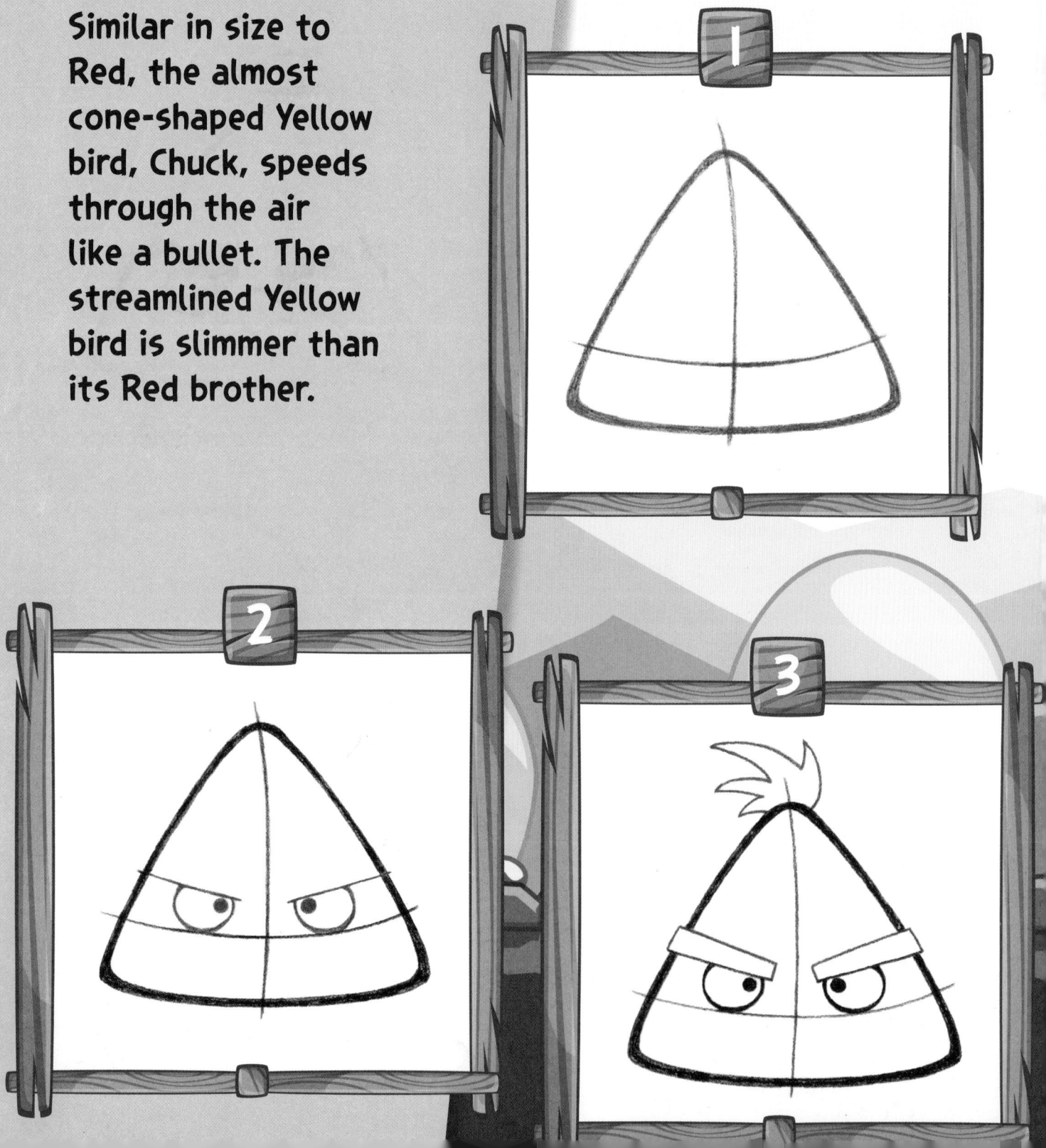

4
5
I'm always fast!

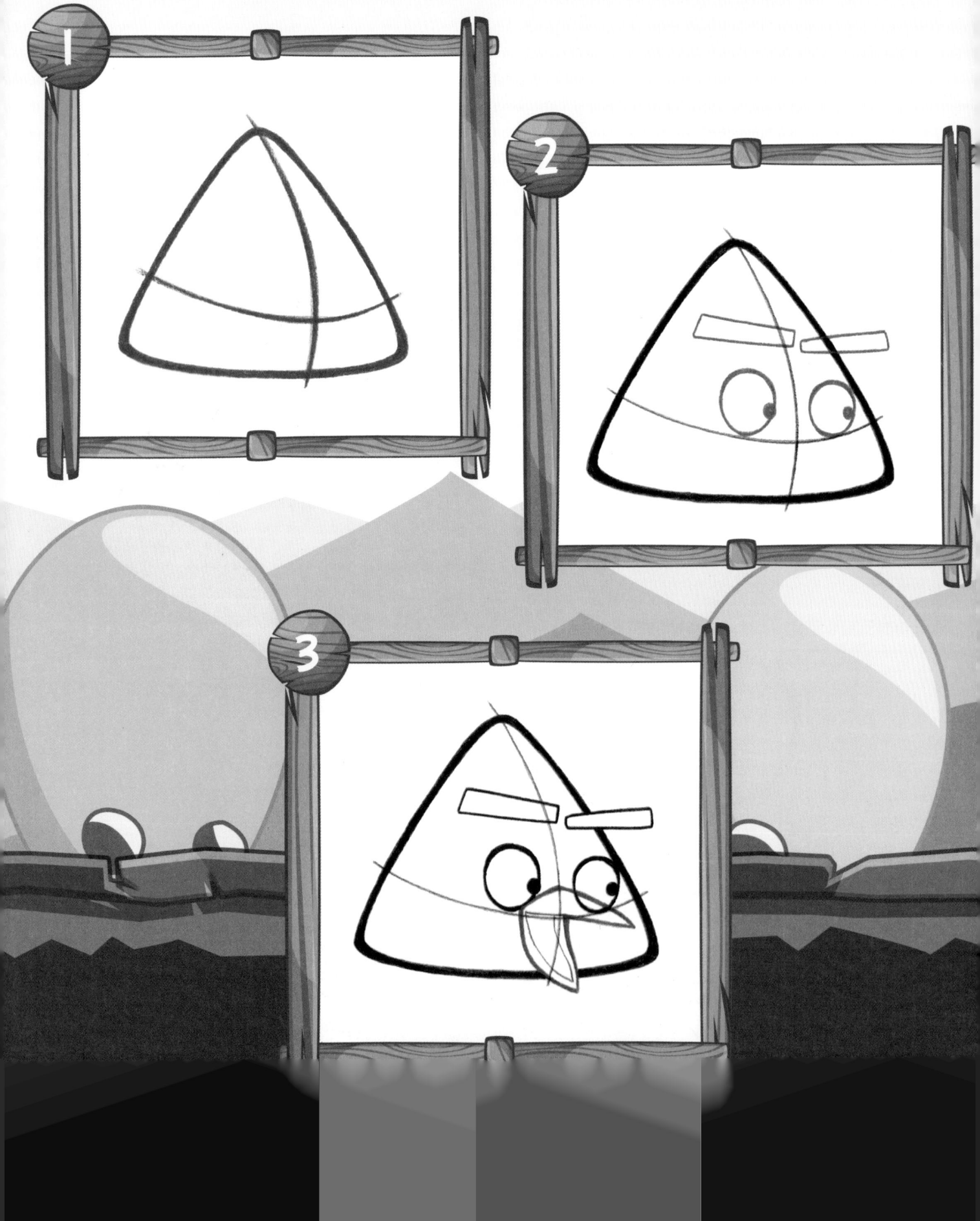
1
2
3

4
5

BOMB

The exploding Bomb is the second largest bird. Bomb has a thin layer of jet-black feathers, which give him a shiny look, almost like a hard outer shell.

4
5
Boom!

1
2
3

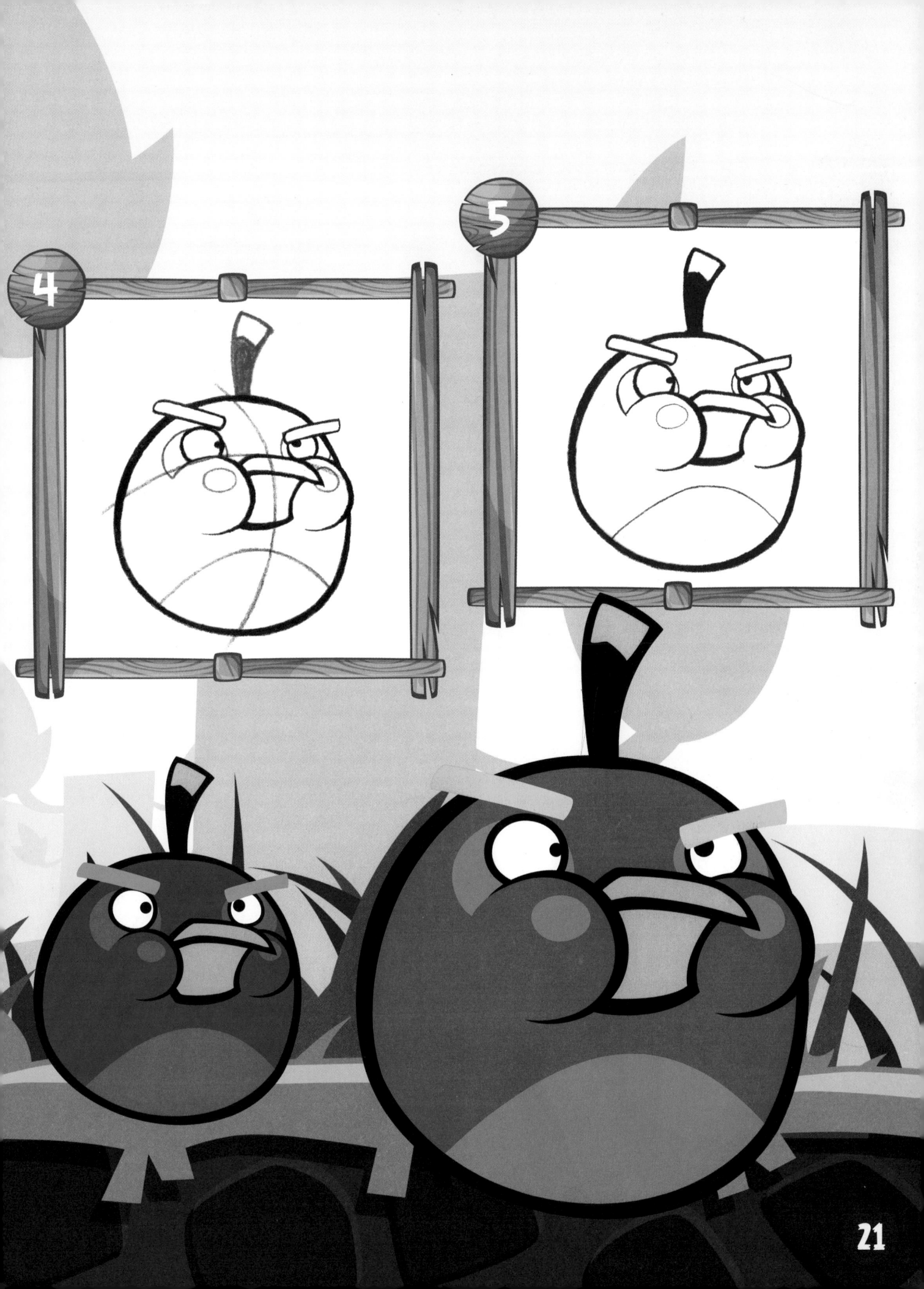
4
5

MATILDA

Egg-laying Matilda sits between Red and Bomb in size. She has clean white feathers and a short, strong beak.

4
5
Drop it like
It's hot.

THE BLUES

Jim, Jake & Jay travel in packs of three. While they don't share the characteristic eyebrows of the other Angry Birds, they are no less determined.

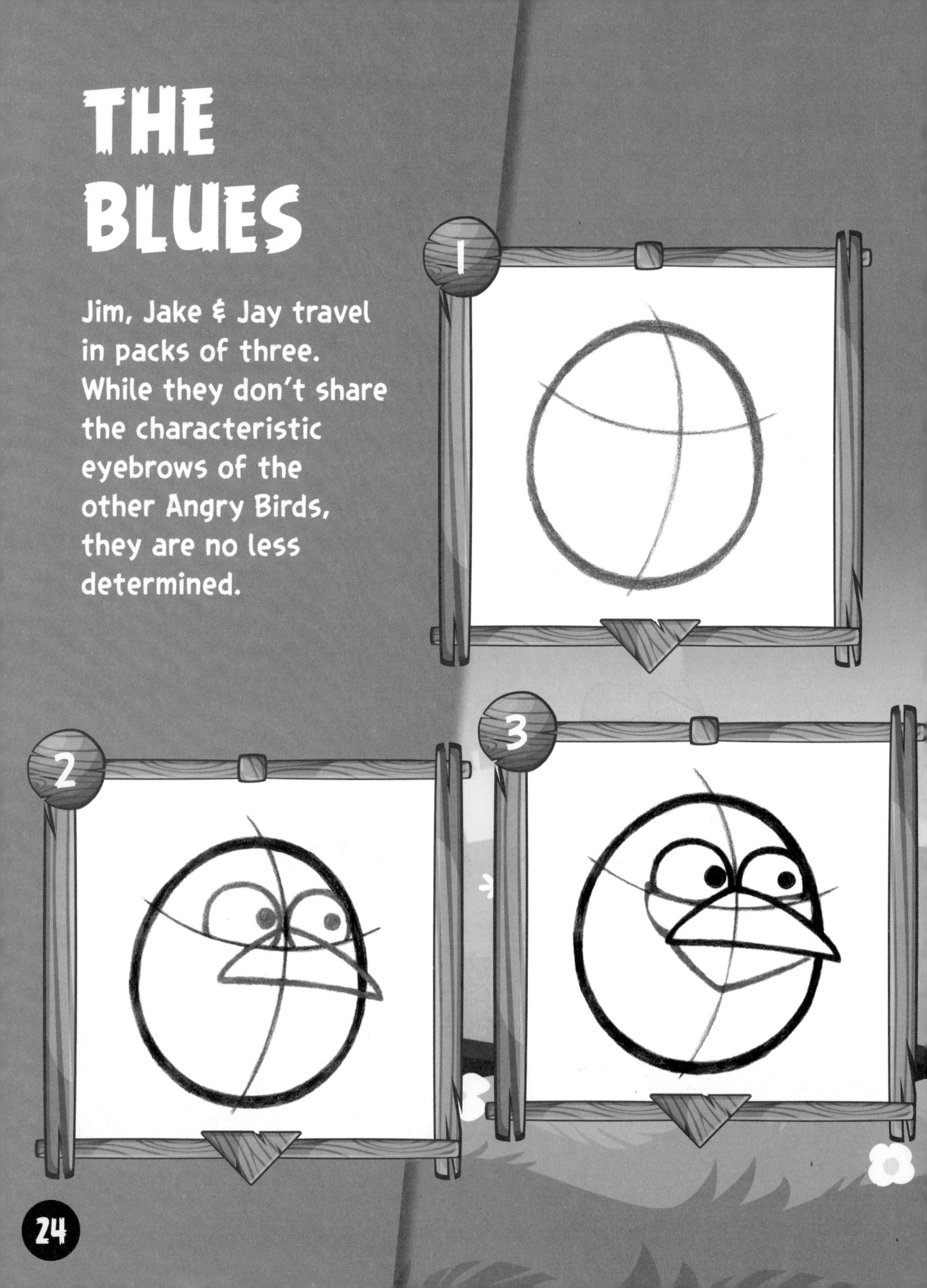

4
5
Triple threat!

MINION PIGS

These cheeky creatures are Minion Pigs of the common egg-stealing variety. They are easily identified by their green skin; short and stubby snout; and their small, round ears.

4
5

CORPORAL PIG

The Corporal Pig is a seasoned veteran and bulkier than the Minion Pigs. The Corporal Pig comes better prepared, and he wears a helmet of shining steel. However, under intense bird bombardment, even steel may bend, buckle, and crack!

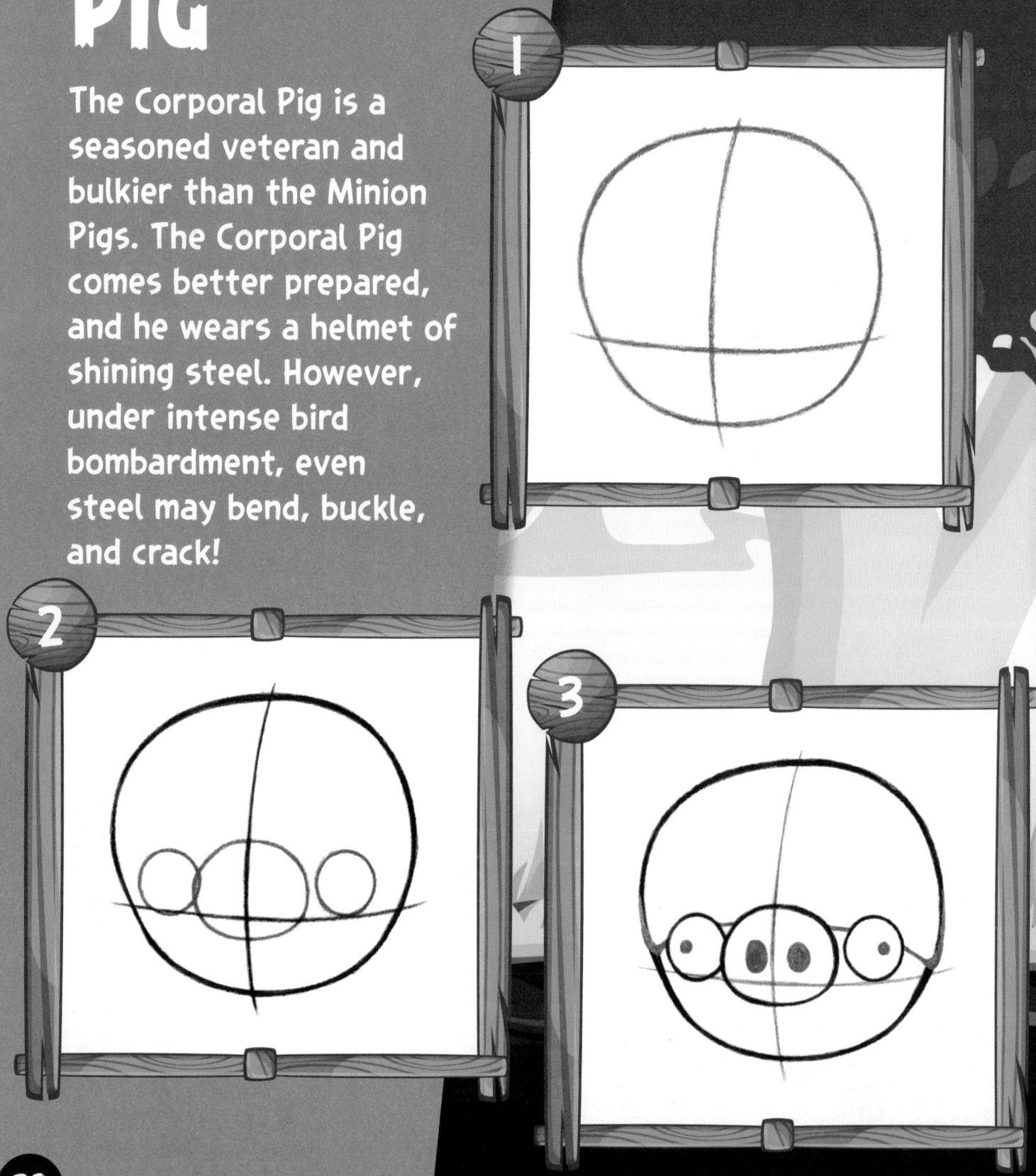

4
5
Pig-poppin' action!

KING PIG

The King Pig is the ruler of all pigs. In addition to his bulk, he is identified from the common pigs by his shining golden crown, adorned with bright blue sapphires. The King Pig often opts for headgear appropriate to the climate and scenery—the various hats and helmets always have been the crown symbol of the boss.

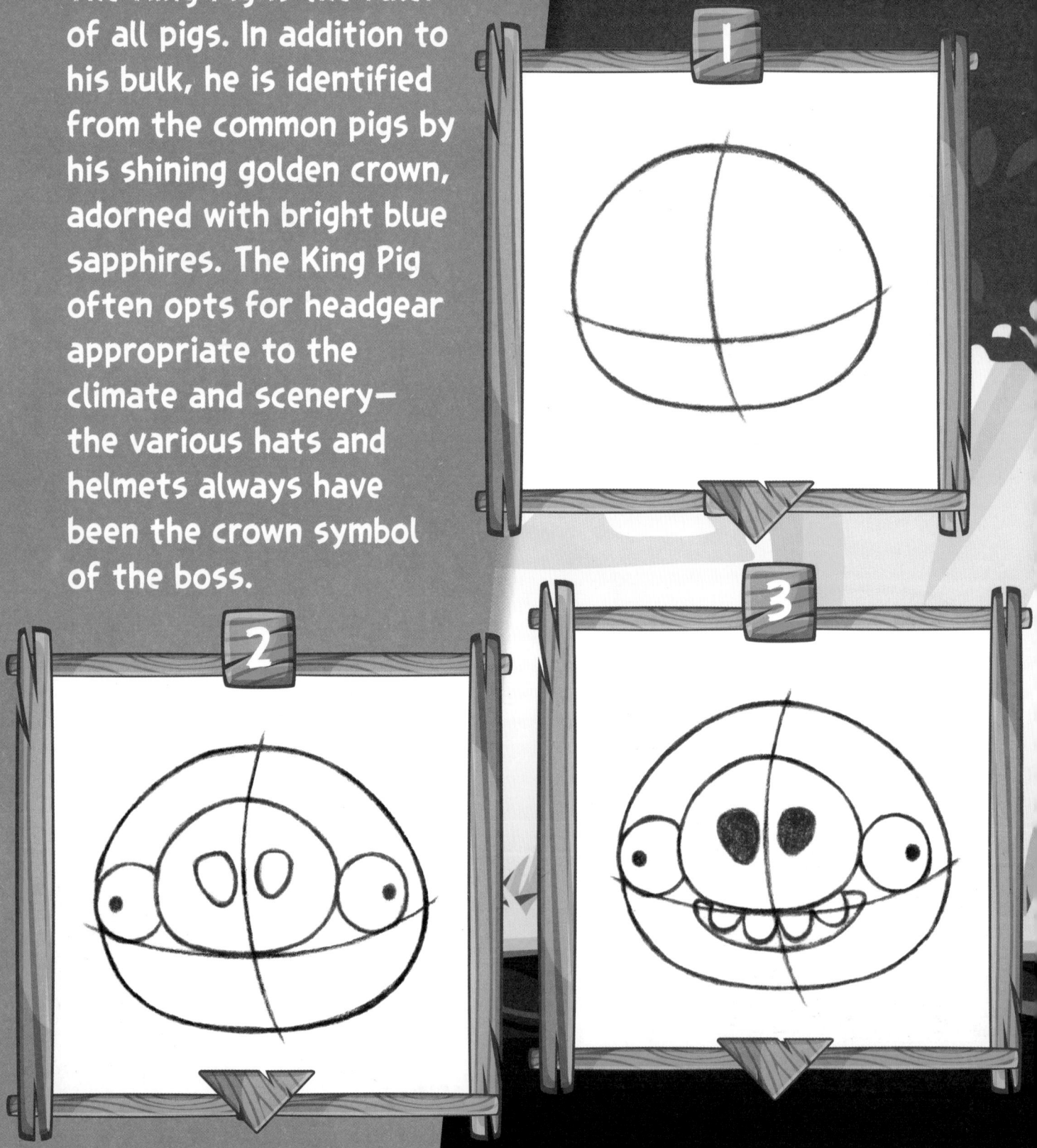

4
5

THE END

Now that you've learned the secrets to drawing the Angry Birds and their enemies, the Pigs, have fun re-creating your favorite levels from the popular game, or create your own! All you need is a pencil, paper, and your imagination!